"The judicious reader will not always a ity of censure, the choice of circumstances, or the style of expression; he will perhaps detect the latent prejudices and personal resentments...but he will surely observe, with philosophic curiosity, the interesting and original picture of the manners of Rome."

—EDWARD GIBBON

"We live in a Visual Age, and there has been a need for an illustrated, or Visual version of Eddie Gibbon's amusing fantasy about ancient Rome. Unfortunately, glassine envelopes were not invented until the ninth century and most photographs of the actual events detailed in *The Decline and Fall of the Roman Empire* are of poor quality. So, I have used contemporary pictures to give Eye Appeal to the casually selected quotations.

All of the scenes pictured in this book are, of course, fictitious, and were posed by professional models."

—ROGER PRICE

"The streets and
public places of Rome
resounded with clamours
and imprecations."

From **THE DECLINE AND FALL OF THE ROMAN EMPIRE**
by Edward Gibbon   **Vol. I, p. 94**

THE DECLINE AND FALL

by ROGER PRICE
and EDWARD GIBBON

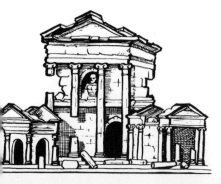

RANDOM HOUSE/NEW YORK

"... the emperor himself,
though he still retained the obedience,
gradually lost the esteem,
of his subjects.
The dress and manners which,
towards the decline of his life,
he chose to affect,
served only to degrade him
in the eyes of mankind."

From **THE DECLINE AND FALL OF THE ROMAN EMPIRE** *by Edward Gibbon* **Vol. I, p. 562**

First Printing

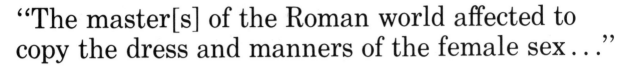

"The master[s] of the Roman world affected to copy the dress and manners of the female sex..."

From **THE DECLINE AND FALL OF THE ROMAN EMPIRE** *by Edward Gibbon*   **Vol. I, p. 128**

"The senators . . . were obliged to provide daily entertainments at an immense expense . . ."

From **THE DECLINE AND FALL OF THE ROMAN EMPIRE** *by Edward Gibbon*   **Vol. I, p. 118**

"The ancient historians have expatiated on these abandoned scenes ... but it would not be easy to translate their too faithful descriptions into the decency of modern language."

From THE DECLINE AND FALL OF THE ROMAN EMPIRE *by Edward Gibbon*
Vol. I, p. 81

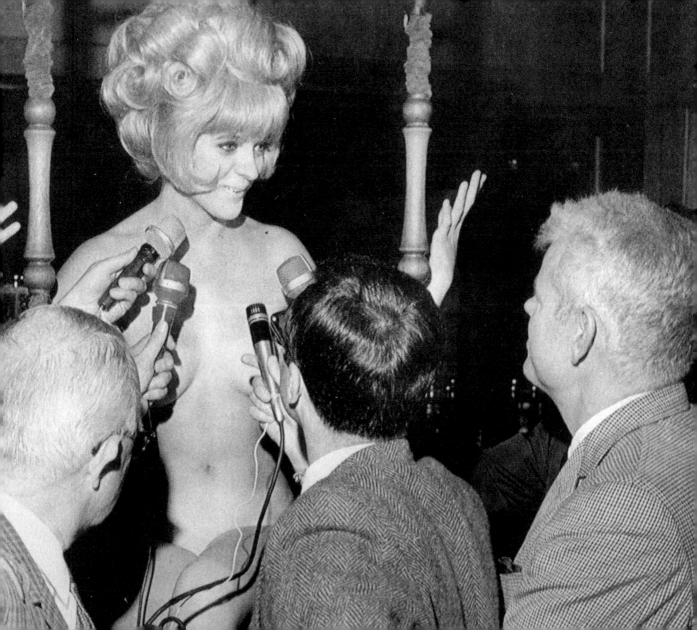

"... their minds
were exposed to
illusions of fancy.
They flattered
themselves that they
possessed the secret
of disengaging the soul
from its corporeal prison;
claimed a familiar
intercourse with
daemons and spirits;
and, by a very singular
revolution, converted
the study of philosophy
into that of magic."

From THE DECLINE AND FALL OF THE ROMAN EMPIRE
by Edward Gibbon Vol. I, p. 340

"Alliances were formed; and armaments, expensive and ineffectual, were prepared for the destruction of the common enemy . . ."

From **THE DECLINE AND FALL OF THE ROMAN EMPIRE** *by Edward Gibbon*
Vol. II, p. 300

" 'Who will ever be found guilty,' exclaimed the vehement Delphidius . . .''

From THE DECLINE AND FALL OF THE ROMAN EMPIRE *by Edward Gibbon*
Vol. I, p. 632

"Fashion was the only law, pleasure the only pursuit . . . the serious and manly virtues were the subject of ridicule, and the contempt for female modesty . . . announced the universal corruption of the capital . . ."

From **THE DECLINE AND FALL OF THE ROMAN EMPIRE** *by Edward Gibbon* Vol. I, p. 800

"... in the prosecution of a favourite scheme, the best of men, satisfied with the rectitude of their intentions, are subject to forget the bounds of moderation ..."

From THE DECLINE AND FALL OF THE ROMAN EMPIRE *by Edward Gibbon* Vol. I, p. 291

"... the Moors and Africans were allured by the hopes of plunder ..."

From **THE DECLINE AND FALL OF THE ROMAN EMPIRE** *by Edward Gibbon*   Vol. II, p. 300

"... the wealth of the state was irrevocably given away to foreign and hostile nations."

From THE DECLINE AND FALL OF THE ROMAN EMPIRE *by Edward Gibbon*
Vol. I, p. 50

"House-rent was therefore immoderately dear ... the body of the Roman people was crowded into a narrow space; and the different floors and apartments of the same house were divided ... among several families of plebeians."

From THE DECLINE AND FALL OF THE ROMAN EMPIRE *by Edward Gibbon*   Vol. II, p. 151

"... the wiser, or at least the stronger, of the two sexes, has usurped the powers of the state, and confined the other to the cares and pleasures of domestic life."

From **THE DECLINE AND FALL OF THE ROMAN EMPIRE** *by Edward Gibbon*   Vol. I, p. 130

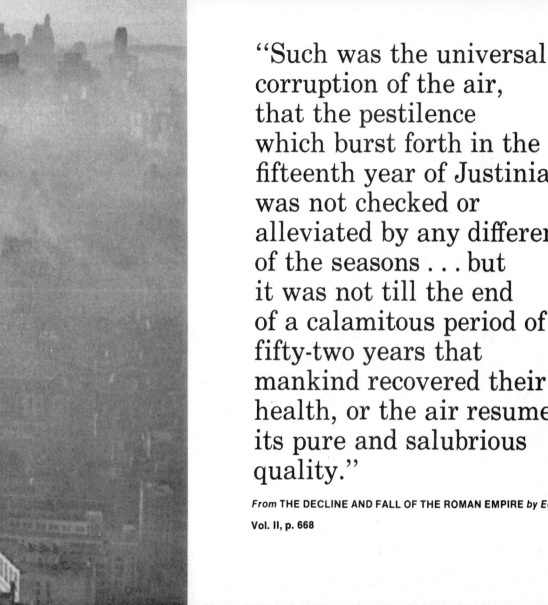

"Such was the universal corruption of the air, that the pestilence which burst forth in the fifteenth year of Justinian was not checked or alleviated by any difference of the seasons . . . but it was not till the end of a calamitous period of fifty-two years that mankind recovered their health, or the air resumed its pure and salubrious quality."

From THE DECLINE AND FALL OF THE ROMAN EMPIRE *by Edward Gibbon*

Vol. II, p. 668

"So urgent on the vulgar is the necessity of believing, that the fall of any system of mythology will most probably be succeeded by the introduction of some other mode of superstition."

From THE DECLINE AND FALL OF THE ROMAN EMPIRE by Edward Gibbon Vol. I, p. 432

"Although the wounds of civil war appeared completely healed, its mortal poison still lurked in the vitals of the constitution."

From THE DECLINE AND FALL OF THE ROMAN EMPIRE *by Edward Gibbon*   Vol. I, p. 107

"It is difficult to form a just idea of his true character."

From **THE DECLINE AND FALL OF THE ROMAN EMPIRE** *by Edward Gibbon*   **Vol. I, p. 95**

"The personal animosities
and hereditary feuds of
the barbarians were suspended
by the strong necessity
of their affairs . . ."

From **THE DECLINE AND FALL OF THE ROMAN EMPIRE** *by Edward Gibbon*

Vol. II, p. 173

"His dress became more splendid, his demeanour more lofty, and he was exposed, under a succeeding reign, to a disgraceful inquiry into the means by which ... [he] had accumulated in the short duration of his favour, a very scandalous proportion of wealth."

From **THE DECLINE AND FALL OF THE ROMAN EMPIRE** *by Edward Gibbon* Vol. I, p. 722

"A law was thought necessary to discriminate the dress of comedians from that of senators . . ."

From **THE DECLINE AND FALL OF THE ROMAN EMPIRE** *by Edward Gibbon*   **Vol. II, p. 495**

"Their persons were esteemed holy, their decisions were admitted with deference, and they too often abused . . . the pre-eminence which their zeal and intrepidity had acquired."

From **THE DECLINE AND FALL OF THE ROMAN EMPIRE** *by Edward Gibbon*   Vol. I, p. 473, 474

IT-204-A New York State
(Rev. 11 66) Nonresident Partner Allocation Schedule

ALLOCATION SCHEDULE OF INCOME (OR LOSS), DEDUCTIONS AND CHANGES FROM FEDERAL ITEMS OF A PART-
NERSHIP HAVING A NONRESIDENT MEMBER AND CARRYING ON BUSINESS INSIDE AND OUTSIDE THE STATE

IT-208 New York State Combined
Income Tax Return 1966
For resident married persons filing a joint Federal Return
who elect to file separate New York State Returns

IT-203 NY State Income Tax
Nonresident Return 1966

IT-204 New York State Income and
Partnership Return 1966 Unincorporated Business Tax

Schedule B (Form 1040) Supplemental Schedule of Income and
Retirement Income Credit

York State Unincorporated
ss Tax 1966

A Special Message To Taxpayers

1040 U.S. Ind

Instr
for Pr
Your
Federal
Income Ta
Return
Form 1040
r 1966

INTERNAL REVENUE SERVICE

SCHEDULE D Gains and Losses From Sales or Exchanges
(Form 1040) of Property

"The old as well
as the new taxes
were, at the
same time, levied
in the provinces."

From THE DECLINE AND FALL OF THE ROMAN EMPIRE
by Edward Gibbon   Vol. I, p. 144

"But the most lively and splendid amusement of the idle multitude depended on the frequent exhibition of public games and spectacles."

From **THE DECLINE AND FALL OF THE ROMAN EMPIRE**
by Edward Gibbon **Vol. II, p. 148**

"Though a stranger to real wisdom, he was not devoid of a selfish cunning . . ."

From THE DECLINE AND FALL OF THE ROMAN EMPIRE
by Edward Gibbon
Vol. I, p. 148

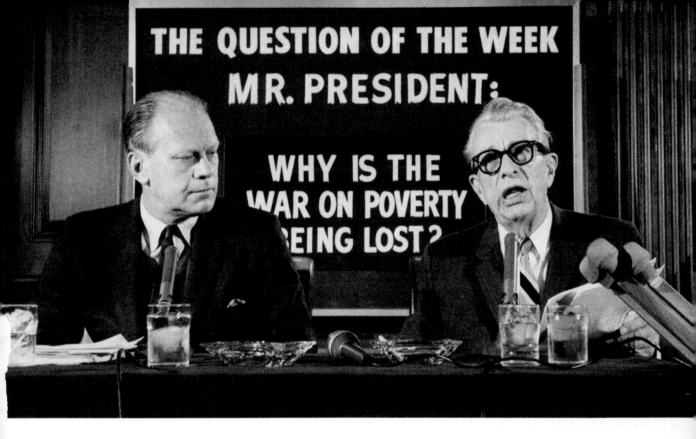

"... the singular happiness of their union has been compared to a chorus of music, whose harmony was regulated and maintained by the skilful hand of the first artist."

From **THE DECLINE AND FALL OF THE ROMAN EMPIRE** *by Edward Gibbon*

Vol. I, p. 307

"The Olympic Stadium was open to wealth, merit, and ambition . . . the profits of a favourite charioteer sometimes exceeded those of an advocate . . ."

From **THE DECLINE AND FALL OF THE ROMAN EMPIRE** *by Edward Gibbon* **Vol. II, p. 486**

"Around the altar a chorus of Syrian damsels performed their lascivious dances to the sound of barbarian music . . ."

From THE DECLINE AND FALL OF THE ROMAN EMPIRE *by Edward Gibbon*   Vol. I, p. 126, 127

"... the senate ... rested its declining authority on the frail and crumbling basis of ancient opinion."

From THE DECLINE AND FALL OF THE ROMAN EMPIRE by Edward Gibbon   Vol. I, p. 109

"Here the fortune of
the day turned,
and all things became
adverse to the Romans:
the place deep
with ooze, sinking
under those who stood,
slippery to such
as advanced;
their armour heavy,
the waters deep;
nor could they wield,
in that uneasy situation,
their weighty javelins.
The barbarians,
on the contrary,
were enured to
encounters in the bogs ..."

From THE DECLINE AND FALL OF THE ROMAN EMPIRE
by Edward Gibbon **Vol. I, p. 218**

"Whatever abilities Maximus might have shown in a subordinate station, he was found incapable of administering an empire . . ."

From THE DECLINE AND FALL OF THE ROMAN EMPIRE *by Edward Gibbon*   Vol. II, p. 302

"In the tumult of civil discord, the laws of society lose their force, and their place is seldom supplied by those of humanity."

From THE DECLINE AND FALL OF THE ROMAN EMPIRE by Edward Gibbon   Vol. I, p. 75

"Every channel of
communication
was stopped or
corrupted."

From THE DECLINE AND FALL OF THE ROMAN EMPIRE
by Edward Gibbon   Vol. II, p. 226

"The provincial governors and magistrates who presided in the public spectacles were usually inclined to gratify the inclinations, and to appease the rage, of the people, by the sacrifice of a few... victims."

From **THE DECLINE AND FALL OF THE ROMAN EMPIRE** *by Edward Gibbon*   **Vol. I, p. 466**

"... he valued nothing in sovereign power, except the unbounded licence of indulging his sensual appetites."

From **THE DECLINE AND FALL OF THE ROMAN EMPIRE** *by Edward Gibbon*   **Vol. I, p. 81**

"The circumstances of his death are variously related."

From **THE DECLINE AND FALL OF THE ROMAN EMPIRE**

by Edward Gibbon   **Vol. I, p. 148**

"The frequent and regular distributions of wine and oil, of corn or bread, of money or provisions, had almost exempted the poorer citizens of Rome from the necessity of labour."

From **THE DECLINE AND FALL OF THE ROMAN EMPIRE** *by Edward Gibbon*   **Vol. I, p. 518**

"But the day of his inauguration was the last day
.of his happiness."

From THE DECLINE AND FALL OF THE ROMAN EMPIRE *by Edward Gibbon*   **Vol. II, p. 301**

"[They were] fully convinced that nothing could reconcile the minds of the barbarians to peace, unless they experienced in their own country the calamities of war."

From **THE DECLINE AND FALL OF THE ROMAN EMPIRE** *by Edward Gibbon*   **Vol. I, p. 286**

"... the tradition of republican maxims was gradually obliterated."

From THE DECLINE AND FALL OF THE ROMAN EMPIRE *by Edward Gibbon* Vol. I, p. 109

Mother Shot
In Gun Cape
2 Men Held

A Queens mother of two was battling for her life last night in a Brooklyn hospital, the result being shot between the eyes during some tragic horseplay, police reported.

Two Brooklyn men were arrested in connection with the incident and arraigned yesterd. Brooklyn Criminal violation of fel... charges of fel...

22 Kids
Cops, Guard

een Toughs Capture
Bus for a Terror Ride

eener Is Seized

A lanky Bedford

CARTHY
ger was seized by detec
the leader of the senseles
town early th

Brooklyn Street Killing

PAUL M
Williams
Bronx

Mug Victim,
Assemblyman
Goe

By
em
ge
ng
as

Hit Whitmore
th 5 to 10
Rape Case
EDWIN ROSS

2 Youths Face
Arraignment
In Prof Killing

Two 20-year-old youths, charged with shoving a Fordham University math professor to his death from a third-floor hotel window, will be arraigned at 9:30 A.M. to-
chester County Crimi-

Teen-Ager Held
In Park Knifing

A 17-year-old youth was held in $5,000 bail in Criminal Court yesterday by Judge Herman
for slashing another

Goes to Hospital
After Muggin

A 45-year-old J
was hospital
after

"... every hour was stained by some atrocious act of cruelty, lust, and rapine."

From THE DECLINE AND FALL OF THE ROMAN EMPIRE *by Edward Gibbon*   Vol. II, p. 170

Head of Corpse

Murder Suspect

...ered

...en Arres...

As Killers...

Doctor Wh...

Delivered Th...

...alts Gun Hunt

...With Assault, Dad Is ...iled

witness

to straighten out the confusion.
Finally, the younger Spann made an
appearance, and the mix-up was clear-
...ed up.
...released the elder Spann
...iling him. He then

trial bond to await trial at a later date: to
...before the hearing the bail
...postcard to the

...Suicide's Poem...

...Wife...

Son

...m on Beating

Daughter

...illed

"Insolent . . .[they] . . .
affected to strike terror
by a peculiar and
barbaric dress — the
long hair of the Huns,
their short sleeves . . ."

From THE DECLINE AND FALL OF THE ROMAN EMPIRE
by Edward Gibbon   Vol. II, p. 488

"... the day of these mystic nuptials was a general festival in the capital and throughout the empire."

From **THE DECLINE AND FALL OF THE ROMAN EMPIRE** *by Edward Gibbon*   **Vol. I, p. 127**

"Toleration was not the virtue of the times…"

From THE DECLINE AND FALL OF THE ROMAN EMPIRE *by Edward Gibbon* Vol. II, p. 836

"These vices which degrade the moral character
of the Romans are mixed with a puerile
superstition that disgraces their understanding.
They listen ... with confidence to the predictions of
haruspices, and there are many who do not presume
either to bathe or to dine, or to appear in public,
till they have diligently consulted, according to
the rules of astrology, the situation of Mercury and the
aspect of the moon. It is singular enough that
this vain credulity may often be discovered among
the profane sceptics who impiously doubt or deny
the existence of a celestial power."

From **THE DECLINE AND FALL OF THE ROMAN EMPIRE** *by Edward Gibbon*   **Vol. II, p. 145**

"But the sentiments
of the East were very

different from those of the West.''

From **THE DECLINE AND FALL OF THE ROMAN EMPIRE** *by Edward Gibbon*

"Enraged by their former servitude, elated by their present glory . . . [they] claimed . . . the possession of the country . . ."

From THE DECLINE AND FALL OF THE ROMAN EMPIRE *by Edward Gibbon*   Vol. I, p. 576

"The minds of men were gradually reduced to the same level, the fire of genius was extinguished..."

From THE DECLINE AND FALL OF THE ROMAN EMPIRE *by Edward Gibbon*   Vol. I, p. 50

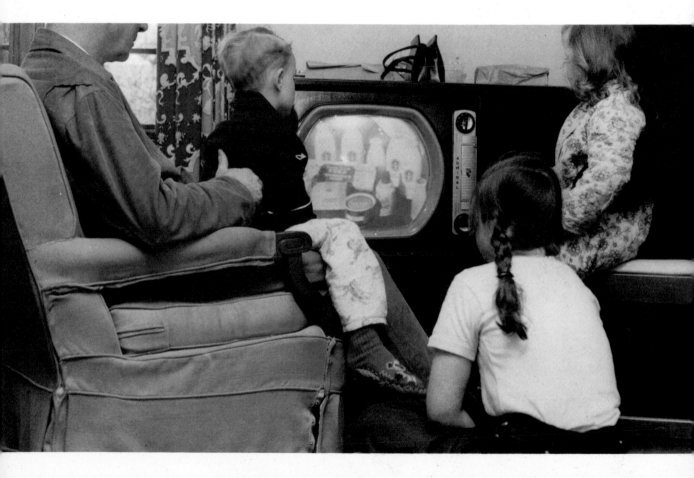

"In every age the absence of genuine inspiration is supplied by the strong illusions of enthusiasm and the mimic arts of imposture."

From THE DECLINE AND FALL OF THE ROMAN EMPIRE *by Edward Gibbon*

Vol. I, p. 762

"...he presumed to save his country without the consent of the Emperor..."

From **THE DECLINE AND FALL OF THE ROMAN EMPIRE** *by Edward Gibbon* Vol. II, p. 759

"When he harangued his people from the pulpit, Paul affected the figurative style and the theatrical gestures of an Asiatic sophist, while the cathedral resounded with the loudest and most extravagant acclamations in the praise of his divine eloquence."

From **THE DECLINE AND FALL OF THE ROMAN EMPIRE** *by Edward Gibbon*   Vol. I, p. 483

"... we must naturally believe that painting and sculpture had experienced a still more sensible decay."

From THE DECLINE AND FALL OF THE ROMAN EMPIRE by Edward Gibbon Vol. I, p. 339

"A life of prayer and contemplation had not chilled the martial activity of Ali; but in a mature age . . . he still betrayed in his conduct the rashness and indiscretion of youth."

From THE DECLINE AND FALL OF THE ROMAN EMPIRE by Edward Gibbon   Vol. III, p. 122

"They beheld around them the wealth and plenty of a fertile province, in the midst of which they suffered the intolerable hardships of artificial famine."

From **THE DECLINE AND FALL OF THE ROMAN EMPIRE** *by Edward Gibbon*

Vol. I, p. 926

"The negotiations of peace were accompanied and supported by the most vigorous preparations for war."

From THE DECLINE AND FALL OF THE ROMAN EMPIRE
by Edward Gibbon   Vol. I, p. 734

"Gay apparel, magnificent houses, and elegant furniture were suppose to unite the double guilt of pride and of sensuality: a simple and mortified appearance was more suitable to the Christian . . ."

From **THE DECLINE AND FALL OF THE ROMAN EMPIRE** *by Edward Gibbon*   Vol. I, p. 413, 414

"[The plebeians] . . . dissipated in extravagant gaming the miserable pittance of their . . . children . . ."

From **THE DECLINE AND FALL OF THE ROMAN EMPIRE** *by Edward Gibbon*   **Vol. II, p. 148**

"[His] generous mind ... was tortured by the exquisite distress of beholding the ruin which he had occasioned, and whose rapid progress he was unable to check."

From **THE DECLINE AND FALL OF THE ROMAN EMPIRE** *by Edward Gibbon*
Vol. II, p. 235